CAPTAIN'S TOWER
(Inner Gatehouse)
built in 1160s,
interior altered
1390 and later

HALF-MOON
BATTERY
built 1542

LMA
LOCK
uilt 1932

BUILT ON SITE OF
ROYAL APARTMENTS, GREAT HALL AND CHAPEL

MAGAZINE
built 1881

MILITIA STORE
built 1881

REGIMENTAL MUSEUM
19th century, but
incorporating
earlier work

KEEP
begun 1122 by Henry I and
completed by David I of
Scotland. Third floor
added to take cannon in
16th century

OCTAGONAL STAIR TURRET
early 14th century

REMAINS OF QUEEN MARY'S
TOWER built 1308,
demolished 1834

CITY WALL

DACRE POSTERN GATE

INNER BAILEY

REMAINS OF GOVERNOR'S OR
ELIZABETHAN RANGE
rebuilt 1577, demolished 1812

CURTAIN WALL

OUTER DITCH

INNER BAILEY WALL
protected by ditch

ENTRANCE BRIDGE
originally a
wooden drawbridge

OUTER GATEHOUSE
(de Ireby's Tower)
built about 1167,
altered 1378–83

ENTRANCE TO CASTLE

HISTORY OF CARLISLE CASTLE

Colin Platt

*The Roman Emperor Hadrian.
A coin found in the River Tyne*

ORIGINS

Carlisle Castle today has a well-used look: the face of an old boxer, bruised, patched and bandaged through the centuries. It has never lost its purpose as a fortress. Two centuries ago, William Gilpin, Prophet of the Picturesque, found Carlisle 'heavy in all its parts, as these fabrics commonly are . . . too perfect to afford much pleasure to the picturesque eye'. It was his expectation, nevertheless, that 'hereafter, when its shattered towers and buttresses give a lightness to its parts, it may adorn some future landscape'. Yet Carlisle has hardly changed since Gilpin wrote. In 1789, just three years later, the French rose in bloody Revolution. Fearful of the same in Britain too, the Government armed Carlisle against the 'radicals'. The castle's military garrison, strengthened at that time, remained until 1959. The final improvement to the defences, during World War II, was the mounting of a machine gun on the keep.

That keep is the oldest surviving building in the entire fortress. It dates to the twelfth century, but was not, even

*Roman decorative harness-
mount featuring Jupiter's eagle,
discovered in Carlisle*

BELOW *Carlisle Castle in 1791.
Queen Mary's Tower and the
Norman keep, viewed from the
city wall. An engraving from a
watercolour by Robert Carlyle*

William II (William Rufus) built the first timber castle at Carlisle in 1092

then, the earliest fortification on the site. From the first to the fourth centuries, for some three hundred years, the Romans kept a garrison at *Luguvalium*. The fort and town they built was still partly standing in 685, when St Cuthbert visited Carlisle. Cuthbert was a Northumbrian, bishop of Lindisfarne, and very much a frontier man. After his death in 687, his cult flourished on both sides of the Border. For two thousand years, from Roman times till these, it has been that same Anglo-Scottish Border which has chiefly etched its mark upon the region. Carlisle, on the west, has checked marauding Scots, as Newcastle has blocked their progress in the east. In 1092, when William II (Rufus) came to Carlisle, it was in response to one of many raids. Rufus 'with a great army went north to Carlisle, and restored the city and erected the castle, and drove out Dolfin [son of Earl Gospatrick of Northumbria] who had ruled the country, and garrisoned the castle with his men . . . and sent many peasant people there with their wives and cattle to live there to cultivate the land'.

There is no trace now of Rufus's castle, which may never have been more than a single mighty rampart. But thirty years later, in the reign of his brother, Carlisle's defences were re-fashioned in stone. Henry I was a careful man, notoriously canny with his treasure. Nevertheless, he gave money in 1122 to the works at Carlisle, which he visited that year and which 'he ordered to be fortified with a castle and towers'. Within the next decade, the city walls were built and a beginning was made on the stone keep. Both were completed by King David I during the long Scottish occupation of the northern counties which coincided with the Anarchy of Stephen (1135–54). David died at Carlisle in 1153. His young successor, Malcolm IV (The Maiden), was no match for Henry II. In 1157 Carlisle and its region were returned to England, of which they have been part ever since.

Henry II was at Carlisle in 1158. He was there again in 1163. What he contributed to the fortress was a stone outer curtain, pierced by a new southern gate. Carlisle Castle, in David's day, had already had its keep and circling curtain. Ringed for a second time with walls during Henry's reign, it presented a triple challenge to the besieger. The Scots lost no time in the attempt. Malcolm 'the Maiden' died on 9 December 1165. His successor was William 'the Lion' (1165–1214). The Scottish king William I was known as a 'brawny' man, not greatly given to political realism. He had been earl of Northumberland before Malcolm's surrender of the northern counties in 1157, and never wholly abandoned hope of a return. For the entire half century of William I's long reign, Northumbria's union with Scotland remained a vision.

Henry I ordered the building of a castle and towers in stone in 1122, when work on the keep began

The Scottish king David I completed the keep and inner walls during the Scottish occupation of Carlisle. He is depicted here with his grandson 'Malcolm the Maiden' who succeeded him at the age of eleven

UNDER SIEGE

In 1173, the rebellion of England's 'young king', Henry II's eldest son, gave William the Lion his opportunity. With 'wild rashness', William led his army south in a war of rapine and siege. Twice he came before Carlisle. The second siege, in 1174, brought him nearer to success than the first. Carlisle's defender was Robert de Vaux. Offered the choice between a heap of gold if he surrendered Carlisle or a brutal death on its walls if he did not, Robert responded at first with brave contempt. But neither the supplies Robert had expected nor his confidence in his men survived the failure of a relieving force to get through to him. Carlisle would have fallen by Michaelmas that year had the Scots not themselves gone away.

William the Lion's surprise capture at Alnwick on 13 July 1174 effectively ended his ambitions in Northern England. But that was not how William ever saw it himself, and the Scottish threat to the northern counties rarely lifted. Henry II was back at Carlisle in 1186. He commissioned a new chamber for his personal use at the castle, and clearly intended to return there. For a decade, from Henry's death in 1189, the citizens of Carlisle never saw their king, for Richard I was away on a Crusade in the Holy Land. In contrast, they saw far too much of King John (1199–1216). In the restless wanderings that characterised his reign, John came to Carlisle on four occasions. John was not a welcome visitor. He taxed his subjects as they had never been taxed before, imposing a huge fine on Carlisle. He was to pay a heavy price for his greed. In 1216, when John's barons rose against him, Carlisle made common cause with the Northerners. The city opened its gates to the rebels' Scottish allies, even while the castle held fast for the king. Alexander II's assault on Carlisle Castle began with the successful mining of the new south curtain, Henry II's latest addition to the *enceinte*. The inner gate fell next and the keep last of all, but not without hard fighting till the end. The toll was considerable and long-lasting. Recording the condition of the castle in 1255–6, Henry III's commissioners told him: 'Maunsell's tower and William de Ireby's tower [the outer gate], and the tower over the inner gate, which were thrown down and damaged in the great war in the time of the illustrious King John your father, were never afterwards rebuilt or repaired.'

THE THREE EDWARDS

Carlisle's long sleep after 1217, when Alexander II was at last persuaded to withdraw, was rudely broken by the Wars of Independence (1296–1346). It was Edward I (1272–1307) whose adjudication in the succession dispute after Alexander III's death in 1286, gave him claim to hegemony over Scotland. Then, it was Edward II (1307–27) whose inferior generalship lost him the field at Bannockburn (1314) to Robert Bruce. Finally, it was Edward III (1327–77) whose higher aspirations for the throne of France allowed

Henry II, from a contemporary manuscript

The Scottish king William I, known as 'the Lion'. A coin issued during his reign

BELOW *King John, seen with a favourite hound*

Battle of Bannockburn, 1314, at which Edward II's army was defeated by the Scots led by King Robert I (Robert Bruce)

accommodation with the Scots to be reached. Carlisle blew like a leaf on these winds.

On 26 March 1296, a surprise attack on Carlisle was among the opening salvoes of the War. In the following year, after William Wallace's shock defeat of the English forces at Stirling Bridge, the Scots were back again before its walls. Neither attack on Carlisle was successful. However, both drew attention to the city's new importance as a focal point of the northern campaigns. Carlisle became the depot for Edward I's invasion of South-West Scotland. His armies mustered in the city; his stores and his siege engines were assembled at the castle; his prisoners were locked up in the keep. Briefly, while Parliament met at Carlisle in 1306–7, the castle became the seat of royal government.

It was at this time, just before Edward I's death, that a 'great hall for the king's household' was built within the castle for such gatherings. Then, early in the next reign, the royal apartments were re-shaped. They were given a tower of their own at the south-east angle of the inner bailey, where they were protected by a separate system of defences. Other improvements to the fortifications followed. The castle ditches were cleared and re-cut. New palisades were provided. The great gatehouse was repaired. Big fixed crossbows, called 'springalds' in the accounts, were mounted on the keep and western postern.

The precautions were timely. On 24 June 1314, the catastrophic defeat of Edward II's army at Bannockburn changed the whole complexion of the war. It was the Scots who now went onto the offensive. Carlisle's situation, through successive border raids, placed it repeatedly in their path. In July 1315, the very next year, King Robert was already at Carlisle's gates. The city's garrison was large – over five hundred men. It had a commander of skill and experience. But it was the weather, essentially, which won the day. That summer, it never stopped raining. Bruce's assault tower – his *berefrai* – got stuck in the mud. Mining was impossible. Every material brought to fill the ditches was washed away in the flood. On 1 August, after a siege of eleven days, the Scots withdrew in disgust.

Edward I's parliament of 1274. The English king is flanked by the Scottish king, Alexander III, and Llywelyn ap Gruffudd, Prince of Wales

Siege of Carlisle, 1315, as depicted in this initial letter of Edward II's charter to the city

Coin of Robert Bruce, 1306–29

Robert Bruce, depicted on his seal of 1318–29. His tunic bears the royal arms of Scotland

Robert Bruce with his second wife, Elizabeth de Burgh

In those dark times, any English victory was a beacon. And the city's defender, Sir Andrew de Harcla, stood high in the favour of the king. It was Harcla who defeated Thomas of Lancaster at Boroughbridge in 1322, and it was for this service that he was raised to the newly-created earldom of Carlisle, just three days after Lancaster's death. Harcla's personal triumph was short-lived. Like Earl Thomas himself, he became entangled in the politics of the Border. Early in 1323, he was summoned to Edward's court to answer charges of conspiring with King Robert. When he refused to come, a party of knights and squires was sent after him. It was led by an old associate and rival, Sir Anthony de Lucy. And it was Lucy who surprised Harcla at Carlisle in his own hall, while engaged in dictating a letter. On 3 March 1323, the earl paid the penalty for high treason, as Lancaster had done the year before. Protesting his innocence, Harcla died horribly on Carlisle's Gallows Hill: hanged, drawn and quartered for his crimes.

Less than three months later, on 30 May 1323, that very truce for which Harcla had conspired was agreed between the English and the Scots. But, paradoxically, it was the resumption of open war in 1332 which brought about the more permanent solution. Edward II was deposed and murdered in 1327. His son was the better soldier in every way. The young Edward III's appetite for warfare and his military skills were sharpened by his Scottish campaigns. Both Edward and his commanders learnt their craft in Scotland. And it was the tactics they perfected in the war against the Scots which were subsequently re-applied with such astonishing success on the battlefields of Crécy and Poitiers. Increasingly too, the prize of the French crown took precedence over every other objective. The decisive English victories at Neville's Cross and at Crécy were both won in 1346. After Neville's Cross, no English army ever invaded Scotland with any long-term intention of remaining there. After Crécy, Edward III's commitment to France became total. Carlisle had seen Edward in 1335, on his way north with an army into Scotland. He never came there again.

Edward III with, on his left, the Scottish king David II, captured at the Battle of Neville's Cross, 1346

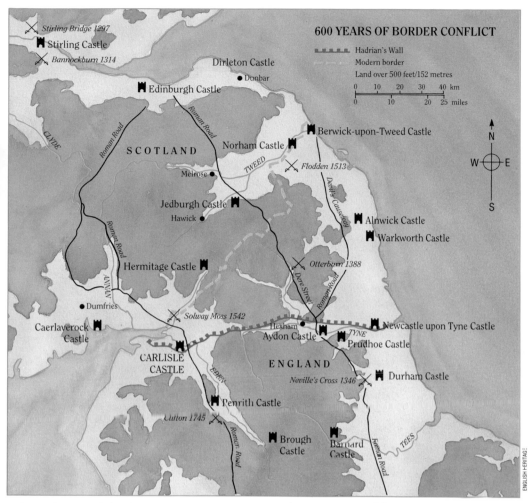

600 YEARS OF BORDER CONFLICT

▪▪▪▪▪ Hadrian's Wall
░░░░░ Modern border
Land over 500 feet/152 metres

```
0    10    20    30    40 km
0      10       20    25 miles
```

× *Stirling Bridge 1297*
◪ Stirling Castle
× *Bannockburn 1314*

Dirleton Castle
● Dunbar

◪ Edinburgh Castle

S C O T L A N D

◪ Berwick-upon-Tweed Castle

Norham Castle ◪

Roman Road

CLYDE

TWEED

Melrose ●

× *Flodden 1513*

Jedburgh Castle ◪

Hawick ●

Devil's Causeway

◪ Alnwick Castle
◪ Warkworth Castle

Roman Road

Hermitage Castle ◪

× *Otterburn 1388*

ANNAN

Dere Street

Roman Road

● Dumfries

× *Solway Moss 1542*

Hexham ● ◪ Newcastle upon Tyne Castle

Caerlaverock ◪
Castle

◪ Aydon Castle *TYNE*
◪ Prudhoe Castle

◪ CARLISLE
CASTLE

EDEN

E N G L A N D

× *Neville's Cross 1346* ◪ Durham Castle

◪ Penrith Castle

× *Clifton 1745*

◪ Brough
Castle

◪ Barnard
Castle

TEES

Roman Road

N
W ⊕ E
S

On both sides of the border, castles commanded the landscape and farmhouses were fortified against attack. Hermitage Castle (above), one of the most formidable border fortifications, was a stronghold of the powerful Douglases in the fourteenth century

MICHAEL HOLFORD

ENGLISH HERITAGE

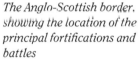

The Anglo-Scottish border, showing the location of the principal fortifications and battles

THE WESTERN MARCHES

Carlisle's loss of status as a forward depot in the wars was made up by its increasing prominence in regional government. The castle became the headquarters of the Warden of the March, while continuing to accommodate Cumberland's sheriff. These magnates required suitable lodgings. And it was to meet this purpose, as much as for protection, that Carlisle's outer gatehouse was rebuilt.

The original contract for the rebuilding has survived. It is dated 13 April 1378, and was made 'between our lord the king [Richard II] on one side and John Lewyn, mason, on the other'. Its terms are unusually precise.

'The tower will be fifty-five feet long, thirty-two feet broad and thirty-four feet high below the foot of the battlement. The gate will be eleven feet wide, and in front of it there will be a barbican, which will be ten feet long on the right of the gate and will turn across by way of an arch in the entrance at the gate to a smaller tower which will be a kitchen. And the barbican will have double battlements in front of the arch of the gate. In the smaller tower, on the south side of the gate of entrance, there will be a cellar,

7

St George in armour, his visor raised, trampling a slain dragon and pressing a spear into its throat

A white boar, the personal motif of the Yorkist Captain, Richard of Gloucester, afterwards Richard III

Two figures in dispute. One brandishes a knife or stick, while the other seizes his opponent's hair

twenty-eight feet long and eighteen feet wide, vaulted, with a fireplace and a privy, and on the other, northern, side of the gate there will be a prison which will be fourteen feet square. And over this prison there will be a chamber fourteen feet square with a fireplace and a privy. And the gate [passage] will be vaulted and will have two buttresses on its flanks, thirty-four feet high under the battlement, and the buttresses will be five feet square at ground level, and will be crenellated. And the tower which will be the kitchen, that is to say facing the moat, will be thirty-two feet high and twenty feet broad on its outer sides. In that tower there will be two rooms, vaulted under the joists, with fireplaces and privies. And above the gate there will be a hall thirty feet long and twenty feet broad, with a wooden partition-wall. And the kitchen will have two suitable stone fireplaces, and in the room behind the dais [the lord's chamber] there will be a fireplace and a privy, with window-lights, shutters and entrances suitable for all the rooms. And all the walls of those towers will on their outer sides be six feet thick from the ground to the arches, and five feet thick above.'

While most of these features are easily recognisable today, the new gatehouse grew in its rebuilding. As finished in 1383, it was both longer and wider than originally intended. It had cost more than anticipated – totalling at least £500. And it had eleven rooms rather than eight. But Lewyn was an architect of skill and experience. What he built at Carlisle was meant to last.

So indeed it has. But Carlisle's great gatehouse, prodigious in other ways, has one curious omission. There

A stag's head, a Dacre badge

*Two dolphins leaping, a
Greystoke badge*

are no contemporary gunports in Lewyn's facades, although cannon by that time were in general use and were even then being cast in the city. From 1380, if not before, there had been a gun-founder working at Carlisle. His name was Richard Potter, and it was Potter's bronze cannon, cast in 1384 and mounted on the keep, which helped drive off the Scots the very next year, when they again laid siege to the city.

The Scots, by one account, had siege guns of their own. And it was in the use of artillery, through the fifteenth century, that they made themselves especially proficient. Carlisle had to be re-armed accordingly. In 1430 when funds were again made available for Carlisle's defence, a substantial part of the recorded expenditure was on cannon, on gunpowder, and on 'gunstones'. Both sides used artillery at the siege of Carlisle in 1461, when dispossessed Lancastrians and 'hungrie Scottis' made common cause against the Yorkists. And it was as a consequence of the damage sustained at that siege – one of the bloodier episodes in the Wars of the Roses – that Carlisle was given, for the first time, a purpose-built gun-tower of its own. Richard of Gloucester's Tile Tower, in the south-east curtain, dates to just about the time of his usurpation of the throne as Richard III (1483–5). It was a modern building in more than one particular. It was made of brick (not tile), newly favoured for defence works. It had gunports at basement level, commanding the slope. High on its south facade, it once carried Richard's White Boar badge: soon to be made notorious by his tyranny. That badge reappears three times in a contemporary series of deeply-carved graffiti, believed to have been the work of Richard's prisoners. The carvings are in the keep, at second-floor level, by the entrance to the two eastern chambers. They include heraldic and religious imagery in almost equal measure, along with the more usual naked women.

PHOTOGRAPHS BY THE CARLISLE ARCHÆOLOGICAL UNT

*Christ on the Cross, flanked by
the Virgin Mary and Mary
Magdalene, their hands clasped
in prayer*

*A feathered griffin, a Vaux and
Dacre badge*

*A crowned lion, Lord
Greystoke's motif*

9

CITY OF GUNS

Carlisle's weakness in artillery was already very obvious before the general diplomatic crisis of 1538 precipitated a reform of its defences. In that year, Henry VIII's former allies and his enemies came together. All at once, France and Germany, Spain and Scotland, jostled at England's gates, united in common loathing of the Protestants. Newly rich on the spoils of the dissolved religious houses, Henry VIII threw money at his problems like confetti.

Among those problems had been malcontent Catholics of Henry's own realm. The North-West had been the breeding-ground of the Pilgrimage of Grace, a popular protest at the departure of the monks. And it was Carlisle's turning aside of the Pilgrims in February 1537 that first returned the city to Henry's notice. But the monks' supporters had been easily

dispersed. It was the next and greater danger of a Franco-Scottish invasion, which really caused alarm at Henry's Court. Thomas Howard, duke of Norfolk, had been prominent in the suppression of the Pilgrimage. When commissioned not much later to 'peruse and view' Carlisle, his recommendations for its defence were taken seriously. Norfolk gave it as his opinion that Carlisle Castle could be repaired at 'right reasonable cost'. However, he saw little purpose in rebuilding the town walls, and instead revived a proposal, made some years before, for a 'small citadel' at the far end of the borough. Between castle and citadel, 'if the town were won, none shall dare remain within the same'.

Norfolk was a man of influence at Court. Such subsidies as were needed were quickly found. Work began at Carlisle in 1540, to come under the direction, from July 1541, of Stefan von Haschenperg, the Moravian fortress-builder and

Cannon on the wall-walk of Carlisle Castle

Plan of the walled city and castle of Carlisle in c 1542, as drawn by the Moravian engineer, Stefan von Haschenperg

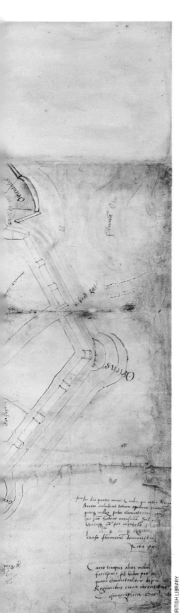

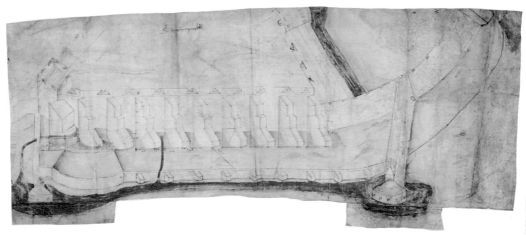

engineer. Of Haschenperg, it would later be reported that he 'is called a man that will pretend more knowledge than he hath indeed'. Such men are well known to us all. However, he had worked since 1539 on Henry's South Coast forts, most particularly at Sandgate and at Camber, and undoubtedly enjoyed the confidence of the duke. What Haschenperg put into effect was Norfolk's plan. The triangular artillery citadel at Botcher Gate was Haschenperg's work. At the castle, his three major contributions are still obvious. Haschenperg modernised Carlisle's keep, replacing its medieval battlements with gun embrasures. He backed the inner bailey walls, to the north and west, with ramparts wide enough to carry guns. He built the Half-Moon Battery, a new stone bulwark, as additional protection for the Captain's Tower should the outer bailey fall to an assault.

Haschenperg's modernisations were neither cheap nor especially well conceived. When dismissed from office in May 1543, the Moravian was accused of having 'spent great treasure, all to no purpose'. By that time too, the Scots had been defeated at Solway Moss, and the worst of the danger was long since over. Scottish artillery, taken at Solway Moss on 24 November 1542, was later included in the armoury of Carlisle Castle. In 1545 there was a bombard at the castle, two serpentines, four brass sakers, nine falcons, nine falconets, and 26 bases. Other guns were mounted in the citadel. But Carlisle was not, even so, a 'town of war'. In 1547 its magazine exploded, leaving the castle's keep 'marvellously cracked with gunpowder'. The great tower remained that way for a generation and more, prompting proposals to pull it down.

Nothing of the kind ever happened. And Carlisle, in the interval, had regained the public eye as the first English refuge – more a prison – of the unfortunate Mary Queen of Scots. Mary came to Carlisle on 18 May 1568. She left two months later, on 13 July, for more secure confinement at Bolton Castle. Her departure was as fraught with problems as her stay. 'Surely', reported Sir Francis Knollys, her custodian, 'if I should declare the difficulties that we have passed before we could get her to remove, instead of a letter I should write a

The north-east outworks of Carlisle Castle in c 1542, as drawn by Stefan von Haschenperg

story, and that somewhat tragical.' Mary had already been a worry to her hosts. While at Carlisle, she had never lost hope of a return to Scotland, for 'the thing that most she thirsteth after is victory'. It was also the case that where Mary lodged, in the Warden's Tower, 'with devices of towels . . . at her chamber window or elsewhere in the night, a body of her agility and spirit may escape soon, being so near the border'. Troubled by these thoughts, Sir Francis had at first been a reluctant gaoler. However, he came to like and admire his mettlesome captive, and permitted her certain privileges under guard. One of these was to go riding, although this he soon curtailed, 'she galloping so fast upon every occasion'.

DUKE OF ATHOLL'S COLLECTION, BLAIR CASTLE

Mary Queen of Scots with her son James in 1583. A portrait attributed to Arnold von Brounckhorst

Another was to watch her retinue playing football on the green. A third was to promenade with her women outside the castle walls, from the south-east postern (just below her lodgings) to the great gatehouse on the south, along what was afterwards called, in recollection, 'The Lady's Walk'.

The gentle image which such scenes evoke, is not too far removed from actuality. Carlisle's fortress prison, from which 'Kinmont Willie' was rescued by Walter Scott of Buccleugh in the dark of the night on 13 April 1596, was no Alcatraz or Devil's Island. The castle itself, towards the close of Elizabeth's reign, was adjudged defensible only 'according to the ancient Saxsone manner of the Pictys and Vandalls against speer and sheld'. By 1594, Haschenperg's artillery citadel, at the other end of the town, was 'greatly ruinated and decayed'. When surveyed for the Crown in 1604, its sad condition was very evident. No better use could be found for it than as a gaol.

OPPOSITE *City and castle of Carlisle, c 1560. In the right-hand corner of the castle (top) is Queen Mary's Tower*

12

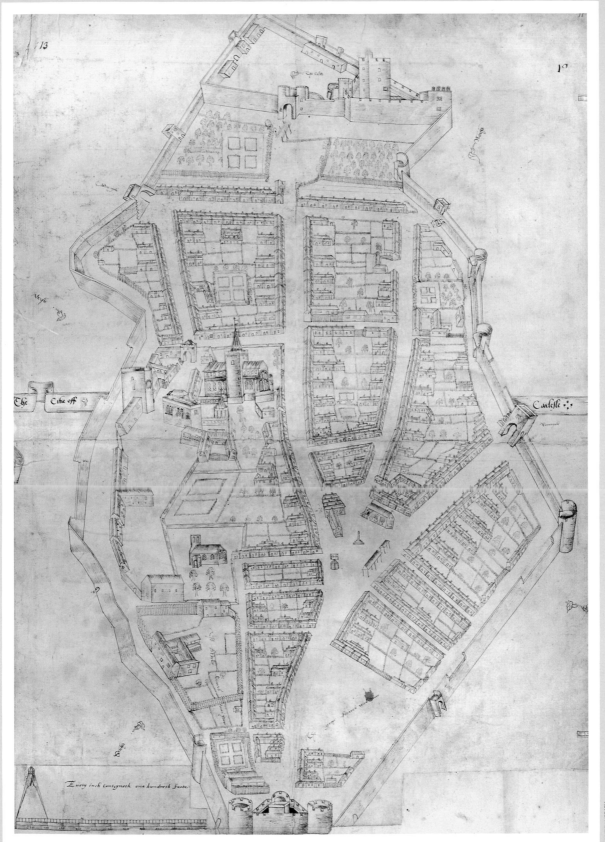

The Cite off

Carlisle

Every inch conteyneth one hundreth foote.

THE STUART LEGACY

Carlisle's border role, on the old queen's death in 1603, might have been expected to diminish at the Union. But those hopes of genuine merger, with which James VI hurried south to his 'new Peru', were never fully realised by his dynasty. As James VI of Scotland and I of England, he saw himself the guarantor of peace and prosperity to both kingdoms. What he gave his Scottish followers was the bounty of England. What he handed to Carlisle was a poisoned chalice.

That was not, of course, immediately obvious. James I's accession was greeted with bonfires and rejoicing at Carlisle. There was a period of genuine peace on the Borders. It was the follies and misjudgements of his successor, Charles I (1625–49), which again placed the city under threat. By February 1638, when the Covenant was proclaimed, Charles's alienation of his Scottish subjects was complete. Three years later, Gaelic Ulster rose. From 1642, in every part of Charles's realm, there was Civil War. The War of the Three Kingdoms had begun.

Once again on a frontier, Carlisle Castle was re-fortified with new batteries, at the south-west and north-west angles of the outer bailey. More guns were sited on the east curtain wall, to such effect that 'were no more done unto it [the castle], the power of Scotland were not able to hurt it'. Francis Willoughby, who by his own account had thus 'so well fortified Carlisle', spoke with reason. When a large

Charles I at Edinburgh in 1633. He aggravated his unpopularity with a coronation ceremony in St Giles Cathedral

BRITISH LIBRARY

James IV of Scotland, who married Margaret Tudor in 1503

NATIONAL GALLERY OF SCOTLAND

BELOW *A simplified genealogy showing the links between the English and Scottish thrones, Mary Queen of Scots and the later Jacobite Cause*

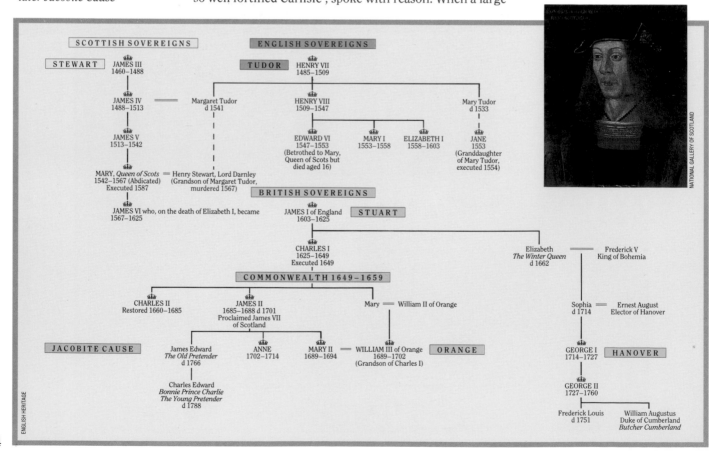

ENGLISH HERITAGE

14

Siege coins minted in Carlisle in 1645 from silver plate donated by its citizens

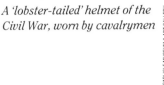

A 'lobster-tailed' helmet of the Civil War, worn by cavalrymen

Scottish army arrived outside the city in October 1644, it was content to dig in for a lengthy siege, finding the king's garrison in good heart. For fully eight months, the siege endured. Carlisle's citizens, melting down their plate to pay the fighting men, were reduced before the end to eating rats. Hope was abandoned only after the king's defeat at Naseby (14 June 1645) had removed all future prospect of relief.

The city's devotion to the Stuart cause left it the very 'model of misery and desolation'. Soon after the Cavaliers marched out of Carlisle on 28 June 1645, Covenanting Scots moved in – as fanatic as any *ayatollahs*. Taking stone from Carlisle Cathedral, they repaired the city walls, patched the castle, and built a new fortalice in Carlisle Market, 'with four bastions, roofed like a house, with holes for the gunners to shoot out at with small arms'. Seriously weakening the cathedral nave, they added to the griefs which, in the view of one contemporary, had already 'equalled or exceeded those of any other cathedral in England'.

Not long afterwards, the Scots had gone, ejected by their former allies, the Parliamentarians. Then the Roundheads, too, were driven out by their old enemies at the Restoration. But the burden of the feckless Stuarts remained heavy on Carlisle, for all the firing of muskets and 'great acclamations of joy' which accompanied the return of Charles II (1660–85). Charles, after years of philandering, left no legitimate issue. And while his uncompromisingly Catholic brother, James II, had no heir of his own, the Protestant succession stayed secure. But then, on 10 June 1688, Mary of Modena gave James a son. Frenzied with 'the transport of the news', Carlisle's hand-picked Catholic garrison ran amok. They cast their clothes onto the celebratory bonfire, and 'ran about naked, like madmen; which', said one observer, 'was no joyful sight to the thinking and concerned part of the Protestants who beheld it'.

BELOW *Carlisle Cathedral in 1719. The nave had been partially demolished in 1646 to provide stone to repair the city walls*

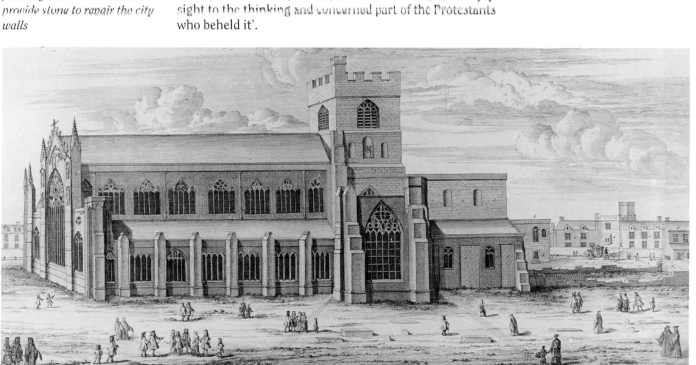

Prince Charles Edward, the 'young Pretender' in 1732 at the age of 12. The Jacobites saw Bonnie Prince Charlie as the rightful heir to the English throne

That infant was later James 'the old Pretender'. And when his father fled the kingdom on 11 December 1688, Jacobitism – a new cause – came to life. For many years, Jacobite sympathies were widespread. And it was Carlisle and the Borders, in the path of Highland armies, which paid the price. Such armies, in the past, had chosen the eastern route, now blocked by a well-armed garrison at Berwick. Carlisle, in contrast, was 'a place of no great strength', and the Jacobites invariably came west. In 1715, in the Old Pretender's cause, the Scots pressed south, leaving Carlisle untouched in their wake. But their strategy under Prince Charles Edward ('Bonnie Prince Charlie') was very different. When the Young Pretender's Highlanders entered Cumberland on 9 November 1745, the taking of Carlisle was their objective. Although 'all the People both of that town and County show'd a great dislike

LEFT *Battle of Culloden, 1746. Bonnie Prince Charlie's defeat was followed by exile in France*

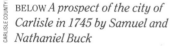

Highlander's targe from the capture of Carlisle in 1745

BELOW *A prospect of the city of Carlisle in 1745 by Samuel and Nathaniel Buck*

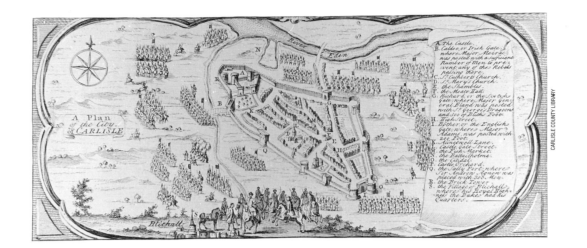

Duke of Cumberland receiving the surrender of Carlisle on 30 December 1745

to the Prince's Cause', there was little, in point of fact, to keep Charles out. Carlisle's garrison was small and its defences weak. The Hanoverian army, under Marshal Wade, was at Newcastle. The Prince took Carlisle in just six days.

Charles left the city almost immediately, to march as far south as Derby. But he was back there in full retreat on 19 December, and departed again for Scotland the next day. Cumberland, the 'Butcher', was at his heels. The Jacobite rearguard stood no chance. Locked in Carlisle Castle, which they had hurriedly strengthened for the purpose, they had been abandoned to defend what the duke at once dismissed contemptuously as 'an old hen coop'. Sure enough, on 30 December after a 'brisk' bombardment, the Jacobites hung out the white flag. Many of them never fought another day. Carlisle became their prison, and it was on 18 October 1746, from the harsh confinement of the keep, that nine were taken to be hanged. Others were sentenced to exile. But another eleven followed their comrades to the gallows a month later. At the first executions, a large crowd of citizens had gathered for the event, which was conducted with appropriate ceremony; 'but many returned home with full resolution to see no more of the kind, it was so shocking'.

ABOVE *Carlisle besieged by the Duke of Cumberland's army, 21 December 1745*

BELOW *Following their defeat at Culloden, nearly 400 Jacobite prisoners were brought back to Carlisle and many were tried for treason*

BARRACKS

The Outer Gatehouse in c 1777. A sentry stands guard on the timber drawbridge spanning the ditch. Engraved from a drawing by Thomas Hearne

Grass grew on Carlisle's walls after 1745, its custody given over to civilians. For almost half a century, all were Chiefs at Carlisle Castle and none were Indians, from the Town Mayor through to the Master Gunner. So indeed things might have stayed until the fortress crumbled, had the spectre of Revolution not been raised. From the moment in 1789 when the Bastille fell and the French crowd knew its power, no English Tory felt safe in his bed. Whig Carlisle, once staunchly royalist, became a cauldron of every kind of Radicalism.

Anti-slavers gathered in Carlisle in 1792; there were corn rioters in the city from 1795; machine-breakers assembled there from 1809; and the radicals were out drilling in 1819, 'with a precision not to be exceeded by regular troops'. In understandable reaction to commotions of this kind, a large Armoury was built at Carlisle Castle in 1804. Filled with arms, ten thousand or more, it was just the sort of prize every malcontent desired, and that no government could afford to leave unguarded. Carlisle's citizen gunners were not up to the task. Late in 1819, while radicals marched the city crying 'Liberty or Death', the soldiers returned to Carlisle Castle. They brought their guns in by stealth 'at a very early hour in the morning . . . lest they should be intercepted by the Radicals'.

Those extreme social tensions, continued by the Chartists, saw little relaxation for thirty years. The military, in practice, had come to stay. The new Armoury was converted to barracks in 1827, later to be known as Arroyo. Next, a Canteen (Gallipoli) was added in 1829, to be followed in 1836 by a three-storey barrack block (Ypres), equipped with such amenities as a library. As the Army settled in, a military prison was built in 1840; a fives court was provided in 1841; two washrooms were added four years later. After 1848, the Chartists' final year, Carlisle's garrison was no longer under threat. However, the status of its barracks had been established by that date. And in 1872–3, when a thorough-going reorganisation of Army districts took place, Carlisle became the training depot of the 34th Cumberland and 55th Westmorland Regiments, amalgamated from 1881 as the Border Regiment.

From that day to this, burnished like a boot, the castle has been home to the military. In 1959, when another amalgamation of regiments took place, the depot closed. But the castle remains the headquarters of the King's Own Royal Border Regiment and it houses the Regimental Museum. Armies are no respecters of the genius of a place. They are impatient with the charms of the Antique. But if no 'shattered towers', at Carlisle today, 'afford much pleasure to the picturesque eye', there is yet something to be said for the barrack square. Spare it a moment of your time. As you tread its blistered asphalt you may feel a frisson still, marching with the ghosts on parade.

The Outer Gatehouse, with a soldier of the 34th Cumberland Regiment, 1835. A painting by W H Nutter

OPPOSITE *Self portrait of Colour Sergeant Dollery of the 34th Cumberland Regiment in 1826, with his wife and son*

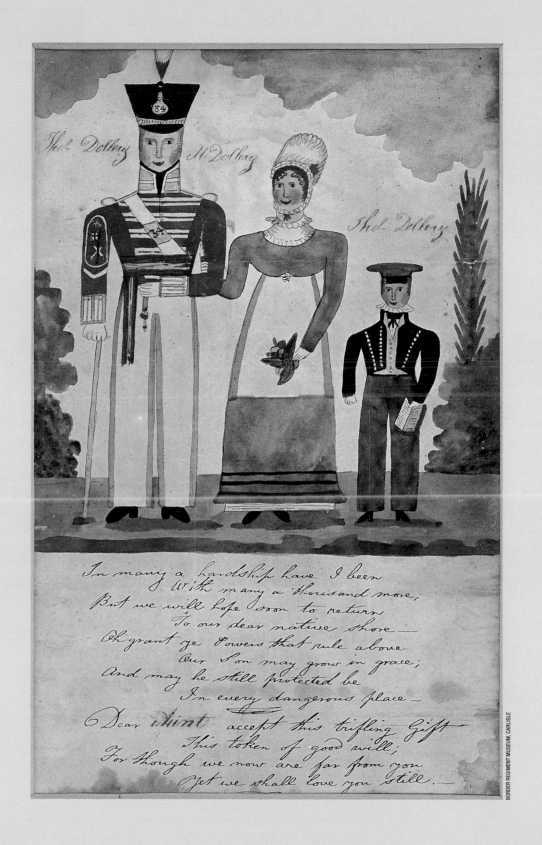

In many a hardship have I been
    With many a thousand more;
But we will hope soon to return
        To our dear native shore —
Oh grant ye Powers that rule above
    Our Son may grow in grace;
And may he still protected be
    In every dangerous place —
O Dear Aunt accept this trifling Gift
    This token of good will;
For though we now are far from you
    Yet we shall love you still. —

TOUR OF CARLISLE CASTLE

Mike McCarthy

De Ireby's gate, rebuilt by John Lewyn, one of the foremost architects operating in northern England in the late 14th century, combined residential quarters for the Constable of the castle, with a role as a key administrative, financial and judicial centre for the county

ENGLISH HERITAGE

OUTER GATEHOUSE

The tour begins in the **Outer Gatehouse**, which is also known as **de Ireby's Tower**, after William de Ireby who stayed there in 1215. The gatehouse was built about 1167–68, since when it has been the main entrance to the castle.

The gatehouse was substantially altered between 1378 and 1383. Much of what you see now dates to that period, when it also combined the functions of Warden's residence, exchequer and county gaol.

The ticket office and sales area probably served as an **anteroom** as well as quarters for a steward. The **steward's room** had a fireplace and a **lavatory** (garderobe) which is not accessible. At the front, overlooking the outer ditch, and originally entered by a separate door which is now blocked up, is the **gaoler's room** which is also equipped with a **lavatory**. Beneath is a dank windowless **dungeon**.

At the back is a mural stair leading to the first floor. At the top of the staircase there is a **hall** containing replica furniture and the remains of a large hooded fireplace. The portcullis housing is visible in the window to the left of the fireplace. The lower of the rooms, to your right, was a **service area**, which was originally screened from the hall. Leading off the service area is the **kitchen** where there are two fireplaces. A door from the kitchen provided access to the **barbican** walk. Above the service end of the hall is a reconstructed **solar** or private room, entry to which is by way of a mural staircase on your left as you re-enter the hall.

Leading off the **hall**, at the opposite end to the service area, a door has been cut through the masonry into another **solar**, which may have served as 'the Cheker Howse' for part

BELOW Re-used as a lintel in the doorway from solar to the prison rooms below, the Roman altar was an official dedication to the gods Jupiter, Juno, Minerva, Mars and Victory by a tribune of the Twentieth Legion

CARLISLE MUSEUM & ART GALLERY

The entrance passed below an L-shaped barbican attached to the gatehouse. The barbican wall walk contains rifle slits probably dating to 1819. The great oak gatehouse doors, replete with iron studs and fastenings, may date to the 16th century, when it was said that the lead roof, the floors below, the county gaol and the doors were rotten and in a state of collapse

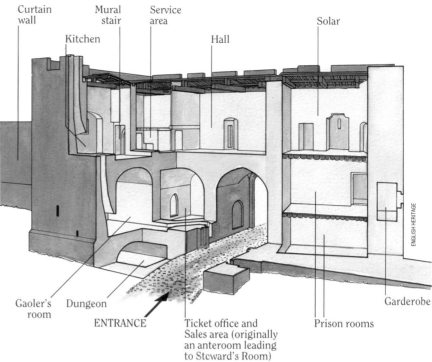

Curtain wall Mural stair Service area Solar Kitchen Hall

Gaoler's room Dungeon ENTRANCE Ticket office and Sales area (originally an anteroom leading to Steward's Room) Prison rooms Garderobe

ENGLISH HERITAGE

of its history. It contains a replica bed, chest and cupboard. The original entrance to the solar is now blocked, but can be seen as a short passage to the left of the window overlooking the inner bailey. The solar is in the east tower of the gatehouse, which retains a number of older and more recent features. The original door lintel leading to a **spiral stair** was formed out of a Roman altar. The old lintel is now displayed here. Some of the stonework visible in the walls is probably of twelfth- or thirteenth-century date, and the remains of a fine Tudor brick fireplace can be seen. Below the solar, not now accessible, are two other rooms, probably used as a **prison**. Now retrace your steps and go into the outer bailey.

On this cutaway illustration the complicated arrangement of rooms can be clearly seen. The main residential quarters can be seen on the first floor over the prison, the gaoler's room and Steward's room

BELOW *Replica bed and cupboard in the hall*

RIGHT *The fine brick fireplace, perhaps one of the works attested in the reign of Queen Elizabeth, testifies to the comfort expected in the residential part of the gatehouse*

ENGLISH HERITAGE

ENGLISH HERITAGE

INNER BAILEY DEFENCES AND ITS BUILDINGS

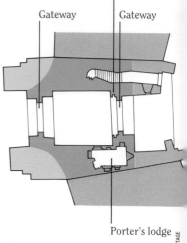

On leaving the gatehouse look to the right, where you will see the formidable bulk of the **inner bailey walls** protected by a deep **ditch**, which was formerly much wider and filled with water. Follow the path around over the bridge.

Before going into the inner bailey, notice the semicircular bastion known as the **half-moon battery** projecting into the ditch. Only the lower part of the battery survives, as the upper firing platform was demolished in about 1826 when the parade ground was raised and extended. The half-moon battery was built in 1542 by the Moravian engineer, Stefan von Haschenperg. Steep steps lead down into a narrow **firing gallery**. Soldiers stationed in the gallery would have fired hand-guns through the gunports. Ceiling vents to let gunpowder fumes escape can be seen.

The **Captain's Tower** is the gatehouse to the **inner bailey**. First built in the 1160s, the outside is typically late twelfth-century in style and has a narrow round-headed window, lighting the first floor. The gatehouse projects forwards so that soldiers could fire upon attackers scaling the walls to either side. It was virtually impregnable. Originally three pairs of massive doors and a portcullis protected the entrance passage. As if that was not enough, **murder holes**, now blocked, in the ceiling of the passage enabled the defenders to pour liquids or hurl missiles at the attackers. A **porter's lodge**, now locked, can be seen in the passage.

The inner elevation of the gatehouse is later in date. If, having gone through the passage, you turn and look back, you will see decorative Gothic tracery which dates from about 1390, the time when Ralph Neville, 1st Earl of Westmorland, was joint Warden of the West March. The windows above the tracery reflect later changes taking place in the sixteenth century. Oversailing the entrance is a second very high arch. This is part of the wide wall walk built before 1545 for the specific purpose of moving cannon around the walls.

Access to the Captain's Tower is available only by advance arrangement with the custodian. There are two floors above the gate passage. The rooms are fairly plain but on the first floor can be seen the portcullis housing and a small chute built into the wall, possibly for the portcullis counterweight. The differing sizes of stone and the variations in stone courses testify to the complicated history of this gatehouse.

Turning to the left after entering the inner bailey, you will see three funnel-like openings beneath the wall walk, these are sixteenth-century **casemates** built for storage purposes. Opposite the Captain's Tower there are three buildings ranged along the curtain wall. At the left-hand end, in the corner near the casemates, is a **magazine**, not accessible. It has very thick walls, a barred window, air vents and a steeply vaulted ceiling, and was built early in the nineteenth century. In the middle is the **militia store** built in 1881. At the right-hand end is the building housing the **Regimental Museum**.

Until the nineteenth century the site of these three buildings was occupied by a single range which included

Above the gate passage of the Captain's Tower were two floors. The first floor, originally containing the portcullis winding gear, was occupied by soldiers in the 19th century. The walls of the second floor contain traces of the original 12th century roof line

12th Century
13th–15th Century

ENGLISH HERITAGE

The contrast between the outer and the inner faces of the Captain's Tower is marked. The Norman front face (see opposite page) is plain and rather austere whilst the inner elevation contains late 14th century tracery and Tudor windows

OPPOSITE *Entry through the Captain's Tower to the Inner Bailey by hostile forces would never have been easy. The task was made even more difficult after 1542 when the defences were strengthened by the addition of the Half Moon Battery. Built by Stefan von Haschenperg, a Moravian land surveyor, the battery would have comprised a double row of guns. At ground level cannon fire could have raked the Outer Bailey, whilst below defenders firing hand guns could have picked off assailants attempting to cross the ditch.*

The ditch in front of the Half Moon Battery was backfilled in 1826–7. Old prints show that it was formerly wider than it is today

CARLISLE MUSEUM & ART GALLERY

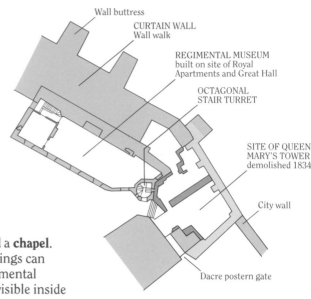

Wall buttress
CURTAIN WALL
Wall walk
REGIMENTAL MUSEUM
built on site of Royal
Apartments and Great Hall
OCTAGONAL
STAIR TURRET
SITE OF QUEEN
MARY'S TOWER
demolished 1834
City wall
Dacre postern gate

■ Original foundations
of Queen Mary's Tower

□ Reconstruction
1834–5

The artist J M W Turner, on a visit to Carlisle in 1797, made a wash drawing of Queen Mary's Tower. It is the earliest pictorial record and shows the elaborate Tudor windows gracing the apartments occupied by Mary Queen of Scots during her stay in 1568

royal apartments, the **Great Hall** and a **chapel**. Today all that remains of these buildings can be seen in the stonework of the Regimental Museum. Substantial fireplaces are visible inside the museum, and traces of sixteenth-century windows are visible on both the inner and outer walls. One of the oldest parts, however, is the octagonal **stair turret**, probably dating to the early fourteenth century, and best viewed from the outside. This stair turret provided access between the royal quarters and Queen Mary's Tower in the corner of the inner bailey.

Queen Mary's Tower, so named because Mary Queen of Scots was imprisoned here in 1568, was one of the oldest parts of the castle. Records show that it was the original Norman entrance into the castle. It was blocked when the outer gatehouse and the Captain's Tower were built. All that can be seen now of the original stonework are foundations and part of an archway with a portcullis groove. Next to this is the narrow **Dacre postern gate**.

On leaving Queen Mary's Tower you will be facing the keep. To the left, the high stone wall, with traces of several fireplaces and ovens, is all that remains of the **Governor's** or **Elizabethan range**, demolished in 1812. This range was rebuilt by Lord Scrope in 1577, as a replica plaque nearby shows. It was here that the Governor of the castle had his quarters in the seventeenth century.

Before entering the keep, go up a flight of steps to the right of the entrance. These lead to the **wall walk**; about half-way up, notice the well which is over 70 feet deep. When the stone castle was first built this well provided one of the main supplies of water for the garrison. At the top of the steps go around the wall walk from where you will get very good views of the inner and the outer baileys. The width of the wall walk provided space to manoeuvre cannons and allowed for their recoil when fired. Two 24-pounder **cannons** dating from the Napoleonic period are still in position. Notice also how the wide cannon ports give way to very narrow rifle slits in the corner above Queen Mary's Tower. Descend the steps again and enter the keep.

ENGLISH HERITAGE

A fragment of 14th century building with decorative tracery, the octagonal stair turret may be part of the building work carried out on the royal apartments in 1308

Originally part of the 14th century royal apartments, by 1529 the Regimental Museum incorporated a Great Hall, Great Chamber and a Chapel

OPPOSITE *In front of the massive bulk of the Keep is a 16th century stairway which allowed cannon to be pulled up to the wall walk*

BELOW *The inscription reads, Queen Elizabeth erected this work at her own expense while Lord Scrope was Warden of the Western Marches*

ENGLISH HERITAGE

THE KEEP

Foundations of the forebuilding of the Keep. The entrance to the Keep was at first-floor level by way of an external staircase in the forebuilding

The **keep** was the original heart of the castle and the first building to be erected in stone. From being David I's royal palace in the twelfth century, the keep later became a 'white elephant' when its main residential function was transferred to other buildings in the inner bailey. It fluctuated between being a magazine, a gigantic 'lumber room', a prison, barracks and armoury.

The keep was originally entered from a **forebuilding** which housed a flight of steps up to a **first-floor** door. The foundations of the forebuilding can still be seen. On entering the keep today, turn left immediately and go up to the first floor. The passage at the top provides access through a plain Norman round-headed door into the **principal room** or **hall**. On one wall can be seen the remains of a large hooded fireplace added in the fourteenth century. A very small room in the same wall may have housed the winding gear for a portcullis. Other rooms built into the walls include one giving internal access to the well.

When building commenced in stone during the 1120s the keep was freestanding and had immensely thick walls. A spine wall running the full height divided the keep into two halves, each of which was intended to be defensible.

The accommodation included storage facilities on the ground floor and two main rooms on each of the floors above. Amongst other essential facilities were internal stairs, toilets, a kitchen and an oratory or private chapel, all built within the thickness of the walls

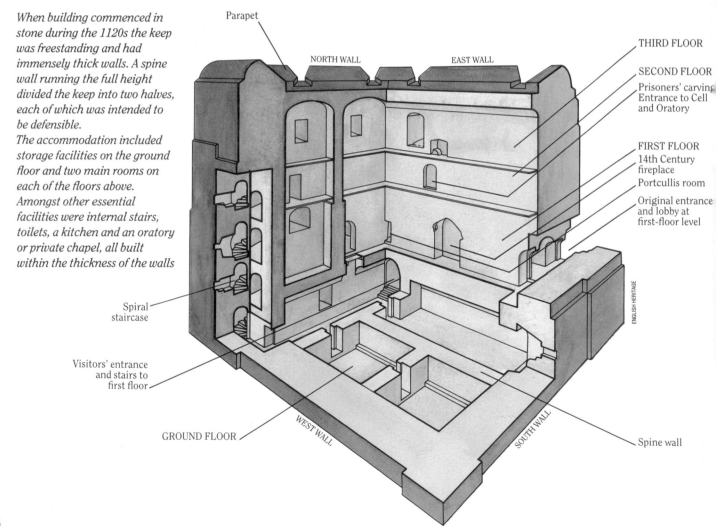

Parapet

NORTH WALL

EAST WALL

THIRD FLOOR

SECOND FLOOR
Prisoners' carving
Entrance to Cell
and Oratory

FIRST FLOOR
14th Century fireplace
Portcullis room

Original entrance
and lobby at
first-floor level

Spiral staircase

Visitors' entrance
and stairs to
first floor

GROUND FLOOR

WEST WALL

SOUTH WALL

Spine wall

The keep can best be seen from the wall walk. From here also are commanding views across the two baileys, as well as into the city and Bitts Park. The gaps in the battlements reflect the changes in firepower. Wide crenels and the wide wall walk accommodated cannon from the 16th to early 19th centuries, whilst the narrow slits above Queen Mary's Tower were for the use of rifles

Leading off the other large room on the first floor is a lavatory, and at the opposite end of the same wall is a straight staircase leading down then up a spiral staircase to the second floor. Next to the staircase is a partially blocked-up room in the thickness of the wall.

Apart from the exhibition displays in the two rooms on the **second floor**, there is a small Norman **kitchen**, to the right as you enter, with a fireplace and a chimney rising through the thickness of the wall. In the same wall as the kitchen is the staircase to the third floor and, at the end, a hole in the wall. This hole shows that there used to be a lavatory in the corner of the keep.

The other notable feature of this floor is in the second large room. Behind a glass door can be seen a **small cell** to the left and elaborate **carvings** made by prisoners about 1480. The room on the right is the **oratory** where King David died in 1153. Access through the glass door is not normally permitted.

The **third floor** is relatively featureless, but there is a model of the city as it might have appeared in 1745. There is also access, up a steep wooden staircase, to the **roof**, where there are stunning views in all directions. The wide embrasures in the parapet were for cannon. An anti-tank gun was mounted on the roof in the Second World War.

Go down the stairs to the **ground floor**. This is almost like a semi-basement today, but in the walls in all rooms can be seen traces of the original deeply-splayed Norman round-headed windows. These rooms were used for storage purposes and, at various times, as prison cells. In the sixteenth century, they were a wine cellar.

OUTER BAILEY DEFENCES AND ITS BUILDINGS

On leaving the keep retrace your steps to the **outer bailey** through the Captain's Tower. The outer bailey today combines the function of a parade ground and car park. It had probably been relatively unencumbered with buildings for much of its history. In 1306–7 it was probably here that the Parliament met in a number of newly constructed timber buildings shortly before Edward I's death.

Although the buildings in the outer bailey are mostly nineteenth-century in date, and not accessible to the public, they are of great interest in reflecting the continuing importance of Carlisle as a military base into modern times. Next to the outer gatehouse and the electricity sub-station are the **garrison cells**, distinguished by their high barred windows. This block, built in 1832, was known as the 'black hole' by soldiers in the nineteenth century. The cells (not accessible) contain some of the original fittings. Part of this range was also a **gun shed** and the barrack sergeant's quarters.

In the far corner, on the site of a former battery, is the **Officer's Mess** built in 1876 for the Border Regiment. To its right is **Ypres Block**, a fine three-storey barrack building,

27

erected in 1836. The southern end was used by officers, whilst the rank-and-file were crammed into the northern end. The barracks were served by a cookhouse, canteen and ablutions, which have now disappeared. Behind Ypres is a small postern gate in the curtain wall. The **Gallipoli Block**, a former canteen, occupies the site of another former battery, the remains of which can be seen to the rear.

Against the northern wall is **Arroyo**, an early nineteenth-century armoury. To the right is **Arnhem** block, a building with a complicated history, but which has served as the Master Gunner's house, as well as a military hospital. In 1859 it was described as 'the worst army hospital inspected'. **Alma** block, a mirror image of Arroyo, was built as recently as 1932 on the site of a fives court.

The way out of the castle takes you over a **bridge** crossing the outer ditch. Although the parapets are of recent date, notice the nineteenth-century soldiers' graffiti on the right-hand parapet. The lower parts of the bridge are much older, probably dating back to the middle ages. The bridge itself was originally a wooden drawbridge resting upon stone walls.

To the left and right as you leave the castle can be seen the **city walls** which linked the castle with the town. Traces of a **turret** can be seen on the walls to the left, and on the right is the **Tile Tower**. Originally a late twelfth-century stone tower, it was converted for use by firearms, as the gun-ports testify, and rebuilt at different times from the fifteenth to the eighteenth century. Access is not now permitted.

A walk around the castle outside the walls will emphasise its strength, perched up above the rivers on a rocky outcrop. In the gardens of Bitts Park around the play area and putting green is the site of massive **outworks** built by Haschenperg in 1542 at the same time as the half-moon battery.

Now the County Record Office, Alma block, built in 1932, is the newest addition to the buildings of the castle

BELOW *Huge buttresses support the curtain wall overlooking Bitts Park. They are very difficult to date with any precision but traces of 12th century masonry can be identified in places. In 1822 substantial portions collapsed. Repairs were put in hand but the effect must have contributed to weakening the walls of Queen Mary's Tower which was demolished in 1834*

Carlisle Castle provides a romantic background for this London, Midland and Scottish Railway poster of 1924